Loose Purls:

From the Recesses of a Grateful Mind

Author
Kimberly W. Walker

Illustrator
Kimberly W. Walker

Copyright in 2021

By: Kimberly W. Walker

Forward:

This book is a collection of poems I wrote since my awakening in 2016. Nothing like a brush with death to make you realize a few things:

1. That I have a voice and I like being heard,
2. Sometimes people value our opinions,
3. That I'm filled with lots of generations of knowledge that was passed on by my ancestors and they'd appreciate us to carry on and share it with generations to come.
4. Here I can share my opinion and not care.....

Dedication:

This book is dedicated to Willie, Demetrice and Dameon my sons thanks guys for enriching my life. To my birth parents and my adoptive parents too. It truly does take a village to raise one child. And to everyone else that influenced the person I became, too the positive and the negative... I would also like to acknowledge my caregiving team and those that I bounced ideas off of. Also Jane, Jo and Iyanna for editing advice, believing in me and encouraging me to continue...

Kimberly W. Walker

About the Author

I'm Kimberly 55, a mom of three grown men, grandma to the best freshman football and basketball playing, straight "A" puller of my heart's strings and a granddaughter I don't get to see hardly enough. At age thirty one, I had a car accident that left me paralyzed from my neck down. The hospital and rehab can spoil you and lull you into a false sense of security. After coming home to a new apartment I would first thing in the morning ask the Lord to make me normal or dead upon opening my eyes. After I realized the incredible blessing I had been granted I changed that prayer into a thankful one. I then decided to live for my children. I knew I had to be the best mother I could be despite my limitations. I still maintain a house, provide for the family, give loving guidance to the guys and supervise my own care. Being home just took on a new meaning. As time went on I realized things were slowly becoming our new normal and easier to navigate and dare I say comfortable. One day I looked up and ten years had flown by. Each child has graduated high school. I also appreciate life more because I'm not afraid to face the next challenge. I even rose to meet one; my counselor wanted me to participate in the Miss Wheelchair pageant in 2009.

Fast forwarding to today, I have learned how to take things in stride, I discovered I enjoy writing short stories and poetry. After realizing the wonderful blessing that I had been given I decided not to squander it further. I have decided to stop living vicariously through my children and to live for myself. I'm learning to speak with the new voice I've been given through writing. **Loose Purls** was born after waking up from another health scare in 2016. From that moment on I vowed not to waste another minute, it was time to prove that I wasn't just an old fool in a wheelchair.

Loose Purls:: From the Recesses of a Grateful Mind

Forward, Dedication, & About the Author

Table of Content

Gone to Soon	4
Anger	5
Little known truths about historians	6
The Voice of the Unheard	7
Our Temple	8
Trapped Inside	9
How Do I know?	10
The Mountains	11
Pride	12
Uphill Climb	13
Children Today	14
Am I a Citizen?	15
How we show Love	16
Conflicted	17
I can't go back there	18
What would you do?	19
December 9th	20
20 year letter: Yesterday	21
Extremely Poor	22

Going through the Motions	23
In Rose's Garden	24
It con't Matter	25
The Cart before the Horse	26
YOU	27
Across the Myles	28
Crave	28
Evolution	28
Free Will	29
In the Words of Martin	30
The Gift of Color	31
It's not Okay	32
The Same Today	33
Behind the Mask	34
Banking for Life	35
Christmas at Home	36
Country Smells	37
Chasing	38
Handpicked Neighborhoods	39
Family Tears	40
Fellas	41
Sistas	42
Am I broke or broken?	43
Beautiful Chaos	44

Don't get it Twisted	45
Love and Hate can't dwell Together	46
Breathe	47
Racism	48
VIC versus VIC	49
Single only Because	50
If and When	51
Going to Return	52
Echoes	53
God Said	54
The Meaning of Christmas	55
Hair don't make the person	56
What am I supposed to do NOW	57
YOU got to heal yourself	58
When I close my Eyes	59
Waxing Nostalgic	60
The Climate is Changing	61
The Many Faces of Kim	62
Unfinished	63
Whatever Happened to?	64
Over There	65
Only the Strong Survive	66
One Hundred Million Words	67

No Fan of Mondays	68
Licensing	69
I want it to be Christmas already	70
Don't tell me there's no GOD	71
Martin had a Dream	72
I Screamed No	73
Because of Love	74
Microwave Christian	75
Freedom 101	76
ABC'a of a Real Woman	77
ABC's of a Real Man	78
Haiku Fun	79
That Little A-frame House	80
I'm sure you think	81
Looking	82
Giving	83
Happiness	84
Life's Tapestry	84
My Assets	85
My Makeup	86
OMG	87
No Regrets	88
Revenge	88
Sunrise	89

Unforgiven

Gone to soon

Too many songs unsung we miss you Marvin Gaye and Tupac Shakur

Many books unwritten who knows the contributions unrealized from Anne Frank and Joan of Arc

No more sliding into home we miss you Roberto Clemente and Jose Ferna'ndez

Not another race to run we miss you Steve Perfontaine and Lilbitluso

No more free-throws to enjoy from Kobe Bryant and Len Bias

No more stolen bases to witness from Joe Dimaggio and Satchel Page

Not more depression to endure Bryce Gowdy and Karyn Lawrence

No more widow-maker's for Michael C. Duncan or James Gandolfini

The list is way too long to remember everyone in this poem, nor is this the most important or least memorable

I listed some of those that touched me, tugged on my heart strings, I understand and miss in a special way

Some I remember personally, some I only know about through my family or friends but meant something anyway

Each one passed too soon before their mission to better the world was complete

Maybe righting the world through music wasn't on Marvin's or Tupac's minds but we felt better when we heard them

Anne and Joan may not have meant to start the modern day feminist movement but they did

We marveled at Joe and Satchel's on field showmanship

We cried when Bryce's and Karyn's light was extinguished by mental health issues before shining their brightest

We were saddened that no more movies would feature Michael or James

However you remember those that have gone before us just remember them in their hay-day and in full glory

To remember keeps them alive in our hearts, so they rest in eternal Peace knowing they changed the space they touched

REST SWEET FRIENDS, FAMILY and LOVED ONES!

Anger

A noun that means a strong displeasure

To be aroused by a wrong

Wanting to exact revenge for even lesser offensive acts of betrayal

Feeling vexed over a nonexistent impossible scenario

I don't know how she could think I would let that be, O damn that was a crazy dream

Have you ever woke up mad about something that happened in a dream, then become perturbed with yourself

Is our subconscious trying to warn us or teach a valuable lesson?

If you ever remember a dream vividly take heed, our brain is always processing; even during sleep

When we have something heavy that irritate us while awake, our minds can rationally think thru things; calmly

Sleep can restore, refresh, energize and also soothe the savage beast

Whenever I got angry as a child my grandma used to say never make life changing decisions without sleeping on it first

Also never decide the future on an empty stomach: A fed brain thinks clearer

She didn't call it "hangry" but that's what she meant

Her favorite time of day to make decisions was 1:00 p.m. early enough to catch the bank and after lunch!

<u>Little known truths about Historians</u>

First and foremost every historical event and individuals influenced all races

Secondly, important events were recorded differently by each region, era and ethnic group

Over time I've gained the utmost respect for Madame C. J. Walker for encouraging female entrepreneurial ship

Most only know her for her contributions to hair care

George Washington Carver is known for his discoveries involving peanuts and cosmetics

But did you know he established Tuskegee's Agricultural and Chemical departments with a personal grant?

Lonnie Johnson is best known for the children's toy the super soaker

But did you know he also worked on the stealth bomber and the Galileo probe?

Benjamin Banneker was a well -known self - educated astronomer, mathematician and farmer

But did you know he also helped survey Washington D.C.?

Charles Drew was well-known for his blood discoveries like separating plasma and that plasma could be universal

But did you know he quit researching for the Red Cross to protest their segregated practices?

I've only opened the door to five prominent black inventors but there's many more worthy of this list

So continue exploring

Happy Black history month!

The Voice of the Unheard

As a baby we learn the art of nonverbal communications

Fidgeting grows into whimpers before the full onset crying that then becomes a shaking scream

All because they can't say I'm wet and hungry

As children coming into our voices can get stifled by shyness or the lack of attention

Nothing can be more damaging than no help to develop social graces

Everyone in and out of our lives over the formative years shape who we eventually become

Children don't see color or gender; hatred has to be not only taught but instilled, ground in daily

Nine out ten racists could not pinpoint that turning moment because it happened gradually from birth

Those that have just cause to fear an attacker don't usually hate whole races just their perpetrators

As we get older, we struggle with acceptance and hormones of teenage angst

Then we try to carve our niche in life and earn the best living we can

Instead of the crabs in a barrel mentality, we should celebrate our brother's successes

Despising our shortcomings shouldn't radiate… it should motivate change

Society doesn't make it easy for advancing; college grads aren't guaranteed positions in their field of study

Most that graduate with an Associate's degree still end up working two menial jobs to make ends meet

As adults we fear for our young men's safety, being black shouldn't put a target on their back

We have scared white people since the beginning of slavery times

They've been uncomfortable with our endurance, knowledge and survival skills

An educated "Negro" is the white man's worst fear; it's hard to break the will of someone that won't bend

Just like Martin L. King Jr. said: **"A riot is the language of the unheard"**

Our Temple

We refer to our bodies as temples but yet we overeat, smoke or drink alcohol

We get offended when someone calls us something mom didn't name us, is there a difference?

Loyalty must begin at home

No one else will respect you or be loyal until you respect yourself

Loyalty and respect are siblings, closer than twins

Loyalty is faithfulness and respect is admiration

We should love ourselves first, treat our temple like we want to live 150 years

If Job can live 900 why can't we see 100?

Loyalty is the key

Love thine own self first

We are truly what we eat!

Kimberly W. Walker

Trapped Inside

Can't recall events of today but know the past vividly

Light dimming on a vibrant soul and memories fading to black

Missing loved ones that have gone ahead to welcome us home

Hating the presence for being alive, vulnerable and alone

Giving up on life, all prayed out and sun-downing at dinner

Regretting the longevity and wishing for the end

Alzheimer steals grandparents too soon

It took my favorite uncle in his fifties

Alzheimer rob families of time, money and love

It turns wives and children into caregivers

It alienate individuals and shun friends

Medicine is baffled but exploring

Hoping for a cure before I can't remember my children and yesterday!

How do I know?

We all search for that perfect someone, the one that completes us.

The three contenders each have qualities I desire and demand...

A sense of humor, common sense and love for me.

Contender one is 6'1" Native American and in my backyard.

Gainfully employed and gorgeous but selfish and petty.

Contender two is 6', unemployed, well-endowed and crazy.

Contender three is shorter than I usually fall for but...

He's a giant in all the areas that matters:

Respect, Humor and Generosity.

Love conquers all!

The Mountains

Fifteen hundred racers at the foot of Aziz Mountain at six a.m.

Uphill in the pouring rain for two hours and then across to its Sister's Summit.

Picking up the pace and my bike for the second leg.

Downhill coasting, dodging branches and gaining speed.

Ahead of the pack and pulling away from closest competitors.

One swim away from victory at a grueling pace.

Ten laps in seven minutes...

Thank you Lord for my endurance!

Pride

An over inflated sense of self worth

This condition affects both men and women

Pride is one of the only nouns with "I" squarely dead center

The worst of the seven deadly sins

It can make a starving man turn down a free meal

We stay in abusive situations because we're ashamed

No other species on Earth suffer from such an emotion

There's more love in the world than we know when we're suffering

Check on your elderly neighbors, the struggling single mother and the bereaved

DON'T let your pride kill you, seek help please…

Someone cares!

Uphill Climb

Born with three strikes already:

Born to a single mom, born black and female

Tenacity may not be a trait that you're born with but I'd like to think my mom's genes are strong within

Those that are tenacious have a certain "stick - to – it-tiv-ness"

This often earns other adjectives: finicky, picky and or bitchy

If knowing what works and wanting the best means these things then I'll wear each with pride

Because to be finicky means you have standards

To be picky means my routine works well and I don't like deviations, I'm not rigid just in tuned to my needs

I may be bitchy sometimes because I struggle to be humble and strong all at the same time

The hardest thing to do is to admit I can't do what I used to; I accepted the wheelchair years ago

Realizing every day that today is more taxing than yesterday, makes being tenacious unlikely

Every morning I awake with a new plan of how to conquer the world today…

Some days I succeed …Hat's off to you girl!

Children Today

Children don't understand what we mean when we say things are so much easier for them now.

Every day you will hear someone utter the phrase "Back in the day" in reference to past ways of doing things.

For instance, TV's today are so advanced that you can program them to record shows, while watching something else.

Back in the day, you choose a program and channel prior to turning, because the knob only went to the right.

Cannot imagine, having to do chores before breakfast or going off to school.

I've heard over and over, that bed better be made before you sit down at the table.

Back in my parent's day, they had to gather eggs and firewood and milk the cow, just to have breakfast.

Today many children never hear or see the word chore, unless it appears on a Spelling or English tests.

Children believe that they're entitled to gifts on birthday, Christmas, Easter and first day of School year.

I was the only child my parents had to provide for fortunately, but still I didn't receive the Christmas spread often.

Today when children write a Christmas list, they expect to receive everything on it, or you'll encounter attitudes.

Back in the day, you had better be appreciative of the things you received and everything you already had.

Although pompous, relentless, spoiled, and unknowingly unaware of the value of a dollar; we can't blame them.

We try so hard to not have them struggle through, or want for, or be denied, and GOD forbid be picked on for lack.

There's a handful of young folks that definitely figure it out on their own, it's cool to earn things yourself.

Because the future always holds somebodies back in the day stories!

Am I a citizen?

I grew up watching reruns of I love Lucy and I dream of Jeanie, I enjoyed them.

I look forward to Macy's Christmas parade and the 4th of July.

I was born on American soil, within the comforts of a territory under old glory.

Does this make me an American citizen?

I possess a social security card, pay taxes and work hard every day?

This makes me an American citizen, doesn't it?

I swore to fight for justice at home and abroad, before ever lacing up my combat boots.

This makes me an American citizen, doesn't it?

According to many nothing above qualifies anyone like me as a citizen.

Like me: A woman, a man of color, an Asian girl, or a Spanish boy; un-Caucasian.

Anything we do, say, or achieve will never be enough for acceptance.

Inventors, Surgeons, Actors, Writers and Politicians who never received recognition until death.

I know they were citizens, but not according to some.

Thankfully the one that matters isn't on earth judging skin color, nationality or loyalties to county.

GOD don't care where you were born, just that you're born again!

How we show Love

In any dictionary the word love is a noun.

The way creatures display affection, appreciation and devotion.

A mother's love is expressed through meals, hugs and support.

A father's love can be demonstrated by providing for his family joyfully.

A child's love is shown by being obedient, helpful and courteous.

Jesus taught love and God laid out Commandments of the ultimate acts of Love:

No Gods before Him and no Idols. Never take the Lord's name in vain.

Always keep the Sabbath and honor your parents.

Never commit murder, adultery or steal.

DON'T bear false witness or covet against another.

These 10 Commandments were given by God as beneficial Laws.

If we follow these rules to live a better life we show God love always and Forever!

Conflicted

Christmas scene in every window of the large bustling department stores but the hometown Mom and Pop shop are displaying Going - Out - of - Business signs.

The 50% off sign in the department stores means last season's leftovers have got to make room for the newer, bigger, brighter, faster and shinier.

50% off at the local Mom and Pop shop means they've done all the belt-tightening, cost-cutting and layoffs; now they are trying to sell anything left on the shelves for pennies on the dollar.

The management at both are praying that on Black Friday 11p.m. totals will be record breaking… big department needed $100,000 in sales, Mom and Pop needed a Million Dollar Miracle!

Three excited children wishing for bicycles, video games, the latest Jordan's and money; A stressed single Mom wishing for the rent and enough money to grant their every desire.

A wayward father longing for this deployment to be over, missing his civilian life and can't call home; tomorrow is the second Christmas away from his growing family.

A lonely Grandma cooking Christmas dinner hoping for a visit from her only daughter's and son's families; with every noise of passing vehicles she hopes.

Displaced because of a fire a family of four loss everything material; knowing they're alive, together, and healthy it's a Christmas Miracle!

A desperate Veteran holds up a sign that reads: I served but can't survive on American soil; Please help my children have a Christmas.

A desperate mother pleads with the court trying to avoid being jailed for stealing formula to feed her twins; her previous employer's store would not yield or sympathize.

A government raising taxes on goods and services but not raising benefits to match cost of living; awarded themselves a 3.5% raise, effective immediately.

Folks trying to be of good cheer says Merry Christmas, Happy Holidays, or Feliz-Navidad; wondering how to provide for their family all month not just for Christmas.

Christmas means something different to each age group, individual and family so no matter how you express the sentiment don't forget the reason for the season.

Look to the Heavens from which your help comes… Thank the Lord for your health, your family and your Peace of mind; no amount of material things will make the day more special.

Jesus is the reason for this Season…

So I feel blessed to see another Christmas!

I can't go back there…

Tip-toeing through the minefield of insult and blame, trying to reach the door.

Avoiding your gaze, but watching your every move.

Planning my departure as I prepare a lovely dinner for two.

How did we get here?

Wine, kisses and roses have given way to Friday night arguments.

Saturday morning cuddling has become who wakes first gets the hot shower.

Sunday mad rush to ready for church, to pray for peace and changes.

Why haven't we said goodbye?

Love can't dwell with contempt and malice.

Is a familiar but barren heart better than meeting someone new?

Wake up sister you're worth more than $750/mo. his half of the bills.

Kick him to the curb… GET A SECOND JOB!

What would you do?

If you figured out the mark you were born with was actually the date you would die in Chinese

Would you live different, would you be nicer, calmer or so be it?

It's predetermined so nothing will change that fate... no other actions needed

Do you live life to the fullest – living on the razor's edge or being cautious?

Do you speak frankly or position every word carefully

Next week you realize your time is limited do you inform your family

Do you start the grieving process or are you finished

The disbelief set in first when you discovered the meaning of the birth mark

Living with this knowledge for so many years can jade or inspire a person

What kind of person did it make you?

Today isn't too late to figure out the rest of your life

Tomorrow isn't promised.... we all have that mark somewhere!

What will your epitaph read...?

December 9th

Leg cramps all night; no school today.

Still tired but famished; big breakfast ahead.

Changes ahead, no more me phi me; baby coming soon.

I'm not ready, unorganized; setting up crib.

Phone rings at foot of the steps; hello, water breaks.

Slow walk to neighbors; mad dash to hospital, hurry up to wait.

Bedridden for 20 hours; excruciating pain, then he cried...

10 perfect fingers and toes; depending on me for everything.

The joy of motherhood!

Kimberly W. Walker

March 18, 2018

Mount Zion F.A.B. Church

Good Morning Pastor(s), members and friends:

Another year has come and gone and I'm still having to deliver my testimony from bedside. I'm okay with that because two years ago it was uncertain that I would see today. Yesterday marked a milestone, it was 20 years ago St. Patrick's Day that I had a near death paralyzing car accident. This made me look back and here's what I see:

> Yesterday I was struggling to feed and clothe my young children.
>
> Today I see three healthy strong grown men.
>
> Yesterday I was working 3 jobs to make a 40 hour paycheck.
>
> Today only 1 check a month but the bills are paid.
>
> Yesterday I realized how far GOD has brought me.
>
> Today I just want to give him all the Praise!

Giving all honor and glory to our Lord and Savior Jesus Christ for continued longevity!

Extremely Poor

Walking to work in a snow storm; no gas in either car.

More mouths to feed than food; Mother eats the leftover crumbs.

No running water; but 3 loads of laundry on the line by noon.

No one signs up for poverty, it just happens despite all.

Now don't get it twisted with being broke; broke is temporary.

Poverty is perpetual in today's I care only for me societies.

A Dog-eat-dog world; Hindsight: no world left by 3020.

Going through the Motions

Actions that provoke an emotional response usually nonverbal but hurtful

The instinctual silent treatment and invading of personal space

Purposely ignoring, blatant exclusion and family forced alienation

To cope you lose yourself in comics to escape somehow; anywhere but here

DON'T worry it fosters your creative side, your gift of gab and hones your writing skills

Early on physical scars, whelps, bruises and lumps gave away the secrecy

Terrorizing can be nonphysical but nervously damaging for years

Paralyzed and as jumpy as a long tailed cat in a room filled with rocking chairs

Realizing your vulnerabilities and weaknesses will never change

Embracing your faith to conquer your demons and gain independence

Sexual abuse is about power for the abusers

Hating the continued reminder but wanting to love her child

Resentment of children produced by the attack often leave an otherwise good mother in anguish

Verbal abuse breaks no bones but can kill spirits

Any form of abuse can leave you barren unable to trust or express love

Healing starts with remembering Jesus endured suffering for us all to be able to forgive

Forgive yourself, your abusers and let go and let God...

Restore, renew and revive!

In Rose's Garden

Five Asiatic lilies in the section named J. Booker Row

They mirror their namesake tall and beautiful

Their robust purple leaves cascade from a vibrant yellow bloom

Deep rich tri-color plumage as though painted by the heritage of the motherland

Along K. Walker grove grows morning glories close to the earth

These peekaboo buds are different colors when open

The pink represent earlier years, the white is current times and blues the promise of the future

Like their namesake they open to a new idea with the early morning dew

On I. Alexander path grows the prettiest pristine white calla lilies

They're the perfect wedding flower, a dewdrop bell shaped kiss from heaven

Like its namesake this lily is beautiful and resilient

Also throughout this garden are birds of paradise, as mysterious and majestic as the bird they're so named for

Rose brought this garden together from above to nurture each other, love one another

In loving memory of Rose Cliffond Alexander we flourish to carry on her love!

It Don't Matter

Your age, race, religious affiliation or sex... neither makes you immune

Blond, brunette, black or gray hair cannot protect you

Policemen or women, singers, actors and actresses have succumbed to this virus

Male, female or gender neutral not exempt

Corona isn't just a beer anymore….

Take it serious or it'll take YOU!

The Cart before the Horse

We all have experienced that moment when we realized grandma wasn't just fussing to here herself talk

When we were young we knew everybody was just trying to control our life

Nobody knew what we felt…how in love we are, they don't understand young love!

He loves me and I love him…. point blank period, us against the world!

Until the first disagreement, pregnancy or first rent payment is due

Playing house just got REAL…

Here's where grandma's voice rings loudest:

Don't give away the milk before he buys the cow

YOU...

INSPIRE me to be creative, loving and kind because you show me compassion,

Peaches

TAUGHT me humility, patience and consideration because you needed me to care for you,

My children

ENCOURAGED me to care and learn about myself because I matter and you knew my challenges,

Dr. Becker

CHALLENGED me to express my God given talent because that's where my passion reside,

Steve Harvey

Made me LAUGH through the pain, frustration and hard times because knowing your story encouraged me,

Tyler Perry

UPLIFTTED me during my low moments because your gospel is encouraging, inspiring and loving,

Shirley Caesar

LOVED me enough to give me a chance at life even though you were a single teenage mom,

Rose Cliffond Thompson

I know this poem isn't the typical black history thing most would think of but it's my history and

I'm proudly BLACK!

Across the Myles

Many cities, counties, states, and villages separates us.

But knowing you're there when I call is heart –warming and comforting.

Although worlds apart we can talk about anything.

You never know something was missing until it comes along.

Age knows no boundaries.

Love can melt the coldest heart and remove all doubt.

I feel a mutual admiration.

Crave…

…Watermelon on a hot summer day.

… The laughter of children at play.

… The mercy from above.

… A smile from those I love.

… Long walks, sweet talk.

Craving more!

Evolution

Change but not necessarily progress

The Wooly mammoth to Dumbo

Natural selection; only the strong survive

Neanderthal man to Martin L. King Jr.

Expansion and industrialized overcrowding

Transformation and adaptation

A Rose growing on the sandy beach!

Free will

God gave us beautiful trees, flowers, shrubbery and the grass.

God also gave us fish in the waters, he gave us fruit, nuts and other edible plants.

God with his infamous wisdom did all of these things before created mankind.

He set up everything that we would need then, He breathed life into us.

After God put us on earth he gave us the knowledge to build houses and to survive.

If God can love us enough to give us these things why can't we love him enough to protect it!

In the grand scheme of things the world has gone horribly awry.

With every generation, we've become more destructive, abusive, and wasteful.

For every new idea of ways to make things go faster, grow bigger, and last longer we seem to kill a little bit more.

The more technology that mankind creates it seems that we lose sight of the beautiful things that God provided.

We seem to be replacing the beautiful shade trees with skyscraper's and banks.

We seem to be replacing the fruit trees with bigger shopping malls.

We seem to be creating faster than we replenish, we should be thinking about leaving something behind.

I love my grandchildren I would love to see them not have to start all over; I want to leave them better off than I was.

God gave us all free will and I don't think that he wanted us to become selfish.

Also under the guise of making things better we don't sometimes stop to think what the outcome will be.

It seems that all we can see is that next great invention that will make us richer and lazier.

Sometimes it is better to work smarter than harder as long as it benefits all things of the world.

Repair, restore, replace, replenish and protect should be the creed, the motto, and….

The prayer that we all should abide by each and every day.   Amen,

In the words of Martin

I say my brothers and sisters don't fret none over the misguided folks

The folks that praise the civil war as a holy war

The folks that hold on to relic reminders of our bondage and still proudly fly Stars and Bars

The folks that think there's only one pure race, white is right

I say don't worry about those folks they know that segregation didn't work then and isn't working now

They know that not only do we sit at the counter, drink from the fountain and ride in any seat on any mode of travel

They hold animosity because a black man help revolutionize astrophysics and

A black man now owns more than 40 acres of the Good Ole Boy's land

You see family since April 4, 1968 we have had a black Supreme Court justice and a black President

Understand brother we scare them because we've embraced our blackness and we're educating ourselves

They despise themselves for mingling their lily white, blonde haired blue eyed blood with ours

The futile efforts of those folks didn't kill our spirit it was just a slight irritant

They to know that a slight irritant can produce beautiful pearls, so I tell you forgive the simple minded

Let them have their Lee and Jackson statues to remind them that slavery didn't enslave our mindset, our heart or drive

You still have to make it to the promise land, you wouldn't believe me if I tried to describe its splendor

Continue changing, charging, loving, striving and living for Glory. It's worth it and you're worth it

Amen!

The Gift of color

Would you live in a bright purple, orange or yellow house?

You know the kind that can be seen from the space station at night without a telescope

What if it's a mansion, with servants and free?

Only rules you can't paint it, hide it with landscaping or deny it

It's yours for free as long as you hold tours, tell folks about it and proudly claim it

Can you, will you accept this generous gift?

Can you, will you follow the rules?

Image now that the house is your body….

Should the color matter?

NO… what the structural frame looks like shouldn't enhance or take away

A house does not make a home

Only what's in the hearts of the individuals within

As long as the colors WE present to the world are NOT:

Reds of anger or Green with envy!

WE should be able to co-exist in this house given by GOD… The WORLD!

It's not Okay

Who is that person looking back through the shattered shards on the cold bathroom floor?

No amount of makeup can cover the scars that have built up over 20 years.

Yet another excuse needed to miss work, my mother or children. I can't think.

From behind tear drenched sunglasses I struggle to see.

I shall make no excuses I did nothing but turn the other cheek.

I love you falls on deaf ears because of a ruptured eardrum,

Love has faded into the will to survive.

The Same Today

I know the obvious nothing will ever be the same….

So I can't cook breakfast I can always order in with your help dialing

Okay it's not perfect but was it before?

YES we'll have to create a new normal

I'm still the same mom that enjoys your quirky dancing and your jokes

I'm still the one that will cheer the loudest at your games

I'm still the worrisome one that will want to know your thoughts and fears

I know you have concerns… I do too

We're stronger than we know yet, we'll be tested…

Together as a family we will overcome every challenge

With faith, determination and cohesive grit, we'll manage

Nothing is going to be the same…we can make it better!

I love you guys!

Behind the Mask

An unknown virus unified the world, reminding us to do what we learned at age four

If we can wash for twenty seconds now, why not before

Six feet of separation now but before no one respected personal space bubbles

Now a face to face meeting is done by skype, we wear masks to protect from our neighbors

The mask can hide a multitude of sins: bigotry, prejudices and loathing

No one needs to say leave my sight, they just put distance between for health reasons

The disdain of a person of color waiting on you at a restaurant doesn't show at the pickup window

Loathing people that are still working; instead of praying that the first responders will stay well

Those that have to wear the mask would rather be able to show their smiles of appreciation

These people don't discriminate against gender or color; they take care of everyone

Wearing a mask and hand washing may cut the spread of Corona but it won't cure the ills of the world

Prayer, forgiveness, tolerance and understanding is the best medicine we all should administer

Love is the key…. helping our neighbors, looking out for the elderly and protecting children

Many say let's get back to normal I say NO let's start anew… it wasn't working before

Let's get back to what God intended!

Banking for Life

I learned I needed to adhere to my morals

I realized early that behaving was pleasing to God

Developing a truthful conscience is easier than trying to remember a lie

Being a decent individual to everyone

Using ethical principles always

Practicing forgiveness instead of criticism

Being a grateful and humble individual

Living honestly, being incorruptible

Always being just and kind

Having love for everyone and being mannerable

Never use obscenities

Live with purity

A quality life can be respectful and have a soundness of morals

Living a trustworthy, undiminished and virtuous life

A wonderful trait to Xerox; flattery is the greatest form of admiration

Yearn to be like Christ

Have a zeal to be a better Christian

Integrity + faith = the best Life's account…

Christmas at Home....

When I was a child in Emporia the town had a life sized Nativity scene

That got replaced with real people every night after Thanksgiving during the Christmas pageant

Each night the telling of the story took on a life of its own

I even played the angel one year.

Our small town loved Christmas from Halloween until 2 days into the New Year

Main Street was decorated with garland on every lamppost

The great tree beside City Hall was lit with any color lights you could imagine

A wreath adorned every front door.

The smell of the live Christmas tree is intensified by the fire in the fireplace until eleven p.m.

11:01 Santa preparation commences: Fire extinguished, milk and cookies put out for Santa

Celery, apples and carrots for the reindeer team and in bed by midnight.

Say a prayer that my whole list is granted and that Santa has a safe flight.

Christmas breakfast promptly at 6 in the morning

No peeking under the tree until fried apples and biscuits

While dad and I ate mom separates some of the presents

Finally nearer to the loot.

I scrounge under the tree and find my parent's presents

Yawning but smiling dad rips open his pocket fisherman kit

Mom says "hurry open yours I need a nap"

I tear into dolls, clothing, shoes, games and a bike was waiting outside I miss Christmas at home in Emporia!

Country Smells

When I was a child I didn't appreciate being alone most of the time having to amuse myself

There was no younger sibling to torture, explore or pal around with

Nothing like entertaining yourself, your parents and their friends to foster your gift of gab and your imagination

One evening after an energetic day of bike riding, running with the dogs and a slice of watermelon I had an epiphany:

While a gentle rain beat down on our tin roof… it was a calming sound, it made me open the window to hear it closely

That's when I noticed the difference in the smell… before the rain the red clay of rural Virginia had a pungent sweet potatoes rotting tang

Even though the scent of the strawberry patch was in full bloom it competes with the cow dung

After the rain began the soil seemed tamed and the stench of the neighboring cow pasture was replaced with the aroma of freshly cut grass

The essence of the roses and mint from beneath my window tickled my nose

Even the laundry that we retrieved before the big drops started to fall, smelled fresher… silly I know, I just never paid attention any of the other times

Mom said air dried clothes last longer and stay cleaner. Grandma never used a machine to dry anything but comforters that needed sterilization

It even smelled better inside after having the window open during the rain shower

I miss the country smells!

Chasing

The inner dreamer in us always wants that bigger, better, faster thing than what we already possess

I "must be the best" on the block, my street, in my city and on the planet

So that's drive

Drive is wonderful because it keeps us competitive, thinking and striving for a goal

When the goal turns to money driven is where things go awry

When you're no longer concerned with improvement and replenishing…

Now you're chasing that almighty dollar

You've lost sight of the goal originally sought, it's no longer fun easy or relative

Serving the corporation not the masses never pleases the heart

A nine to five dream has now become a nightmare

Dreaming of simpler times

You buy a lottery ticket and win $2500…. is it just that easy!

Oh boy your new chase is on!

Handpicked Neighborhoods

The efficiency on 14th near the University perfect for office space

That tiny cottage on Riverside next to the big 10 room Victorian

The cute cookie-cutter two bedroom at the end of the cul-de-sac on Short Caroline

Even the two bedroom trailer on Bitternut lane

Each place held its own charm, served its purpose and worked because it was necessary

But none felt like home more than the two bedroom apartment in Whitewood

I chose every address listed above except Whitewood… it was assigned but perfect

Nothing like moving because you want to

NOT having to worry that something would crawl in from beneath, slither under or break in

It was affordable, freshly renovated and mine

I'm a put down roots kind of person… find a place and stay awhile

Eleven years at Whitewood and now twenty- two at current complex

Recently renovated bathroom… starting to feel like home!

Family Tears

When family tears fall who's there to offer a shoulder?

We're all going to feel the salt of family tears at some point

Our parents will grow old, get ill and pass away hopefully you and your siblings can comfort each other

I grew up as an only child

When a boyfriend turns into someone you don't know the tears flow silently behind a painted on smile

No time to sulk… bills to pay

Finally someone to love me unconditionally, he's perfect, so tiny and needy; tears of terror

We're alone and homeless

Fighting back tears of depression in daylight and bawling every night because life hits hard and repeatedly

Missing any kind of stability

Trying to understand me and find peace before the next wave; I made it… tears of joy

Just working and living

More children, two deadbeat dads, court appearances and illnesses; tears of fear

Turned to God

The tears still flow while talking to Jesus but when I arise I know I can make it

I never shed any tears over my accident because I knew that God brought me thru

My children bring me to tears often in every way; faith tested but love prevails

I refuse to let anyone steal my joy, peace and sanity

Praying hard today!

Fellas

After a conversation with my son's friend I now know they could benefit from Grandma's wisdom also

I've heard her voice echoing these rules to my uncle enough to share confidently

First and foremost never call her something you don't want someone to call your mother

Love her gently, compassionately, wholeheartedly and only her

Be her prince, her knight in shining armor but be confident enough to let her shine too

Love is a two-way-street meant to be traveled together

Shower each other with affection and listen to each other

Be respectful… don't do anything you wouldn't want your sister doing

Be honest, caring and forthright… don't use and abuse

DON'T try to hold on to someone who doesn't want to be held

Always wear a watch so you can be on time and know when it's time to leave

Every king will have a queen someday but until she finds you be your best you

Guys remember your heart matters too!

Sistas

NOT only are sisters our female siblings but …

A good big sis will protect and guide her younger siblings

Two sisters can be a force to be reckoned with

Sometimes sisters share a bond so deeply they can complete each other's thoughts

On the other hand some sisters could kill each other daily but won't let anyone else kill the other one

I think the best sisters are S-I-S-T-A-S:

S= Sincere friends

I= Individual's that have your back

S= someone to share your thoughts with

T= true blue

A= attentive

S= similar taste

These people can be family but don't necessarily need to be related…

Am I broke or Broken?

In my checking account at any given day after the 15th there's usually less than fifty dollars

By many accountings, I'm broke

I say NO, I'm not…. I've never once gone hungry, without electricity or been without medication

I may have had to wait on a want but never on a need…. that's the riches of GOD!

I'm a shopaholic and in debt up to my ears, but does that mean I'm broke

I hear you screaming YES

A girl can never have too many clothes or shoes

Yes maybe I'm trying to replace the old, the worn out or the past.

Which brings up the second question… am I broken?

Never… badly bent maybe

Between accidents, many illnesses and multiple surgeries….my body has been weakened

My mind has been attacked five or more times by illnesses

The Devil will try to shake you and break you by any means necessary

Kidney stones, Gall stones and even encephalitis

He even stole my life twice on the same day…

Thankfully GOD isn't through with ME yet…Amen!

Beautiful Chaos

Born September 25, 2020 at 7:17p.m....amidst a pandemic

Four pounds and eight ounces of pure heart stealing love

Already entangling everyone's feelings with her cute devilish smile

Now a father's joy, soon her boyfriend will become his worst nightmare

Moving out of the way for a sibling, holding head up by two months

Nothing "preemie" about this "Little Missy's game" trying to talk at three months

Spoiled rotten, opinionated and understands how to command attention

Don't want to sleep in crib.... loves daddy's shoulder to catch some Zzzz's

No matter the amount of weight gained, the difficulties during the pregnancy

Forgotten is the frequent bathroom trips, the long labor and the pain of childbirth

All is forgiven with the first cry into the world, it's apparent who rules the roost!

Always the baby, welcome to our lives.....

Norah!

DON'T get it Twisted

Because I'm quiet don't mean I'm stupid

I just have enough sense to listen more and talk only when necessary

I speak when spoken to, when I have a question and when I need you to leave me alone

I'm not mean, I just enjoy peace and quiet

Because I don't join in doesn't mean I'm antisocial

It's not always necessary to be the life of the party

Teddy Roosevelt said "Speak softly and carry a big stick"

He meant be quiet and let your actions speak for you

It's when your actions are idiotic they scream the loudest

Think before you speak… You'll have less to apologize for!

LOVE and HATE can't dwell together...

ACCEPT that love shouldn't hurt...

BELIEVE that friends and family do care...

CONSIDER staying with someone else until you're stronger...

DON'T make excuses for your abuser....

EMPLOY all avenues of helpful resources...

FORGIVE but never forget...

GIVE it over to God...

HEALING starts in the heart...

INSPIRE yourself...

JESUS forgave his enemies...

KNOW that you're worthy...

LIKE yourself enough to leave...

MOVE in positive circles...

NEVER expect someone to change upon request...

OBTAIN the necessary help...

PRAY for strength and closure...

QUICKLY replace negative friends...

RESEARCH the sources that can help...

STAY positive and ever vigilant...

TRAVEL in new groups...

UNDERSTAND that your abuser is hurting from a different place than you...

VIOLENCE takes many forms...

WISHING will not change the situation...

XRAYS and documentation for court and police...

YOU have to love yourself enough to live...

ZIPPED lips lead to death....

SOMETHING will cause one of YOU to SNAP eventually. Seek help please!

Breathe

What do you do after running that race; win or not …

When the last child walks across that stage and turns that tassel….

After that last payment is made on your mortgage and you burn the loan papers…

You get the news that you're in remission again….

Looking back over my life I must thank God for the good and even more for the bad

I'm blessed to still be here to write about me and my friend experiences

So after the day has finished, I say thank you Lord!

I lay down and…**Breathe!**

Racism

I was at a school play with friends

When I happened upon a young boy sobbing alone

Like any concerned parent would, I asked if he was okay

He said "I don't know where my family is and I need to go"

The second part was easier than finding his family

So like the wind we took off towards the restrooms

There's a line at the men's room yes the men's

He started doing the "pee-pee dance" and crossing his legs

So we dashed into the ladies room without hesitation

While he was in the stall a woman kept looking at me side eyed

The obvious differences in our skin tone kept me silent

She had questions for the young man when he emerged

He explained that I helped him find the bathroom

She insisted on helping him find his parents

I lagged back but ever present because I didn't know her or trust her

I believe the feeling was mutual

We eventually found his older brother near the spot I first seen him

After the reunion she tried to claim I was acting suspiciously….

That's why she intervened

The youngster whispered in his brother's ear

Just then his white father and black mother walked up and thanked me.

Because his biological white mother was abusive….He would've never trusted that lady alone!

VIC versus VIC

VIC and VIC live inside all of us.

They are exactly opposite of each other.

You can't have one without the other.

I will explain why they go together.

Every day each one of us deals with the VICS.

We decide in every circumstance which option we are going to do.

Sometimes the consequences are vastly different from what we wanted.

This is where we are tested, and VIC and VIC, show up daily.

You see the first VIC has to show up to make us decide to fight or fold.

You see the VIC I am talking about is the word victim.

I may have been a victim of a car accident, but it does not define my life.

Although tragic, and crippling it did not kill me; so I have more work to do.

Now I can introduce you to VIC number two, This VIC is harder to achieve.

This VIC will test our faith, and our stamina.

This VIC is going to take determination, will power, and a lot of prayer.

You see this VIC that I have been talking about is called Victory…Amen!

<u>Single only because…</u>

God knows the craziness you've endured all for the sake of love

Be patient my sister, hold on my brother,

Your perfect union is being cultivated

We all need the lessons of life to appreciate the good times

We recognize the flaws of our actions when they hurt others and don't want to meet karma

Love is a special sentiment and should be cherished and protected

God is grooming you for that perfect partnership

God is working on you and yours together even though you've never met

Two hearts that share one heartbeat!

If and When

If I share my thoughts with you, will you listen?

When I share my thoughts, I want you to hear me.

If I give you my time will you value it?

When I give you my time, I consider you both precious.

If I give you my heart, will you cherish it for all Times?

When I give you my heart it will be forever.

Kimberly W. Walker

Going to return

No pot of gold, shamrock or leprechauns; just strange luck.

Thirty-seven miles per hour on a straight-away; tumbling over and over.

Airlifted to hospital, terrified of flying; heart racing.

Halo screws boing into my skull, weighed down; no movement alone.

Learning to sit up, finding my balance; blown over like a feather.

Daily therapy, seating evaluation and new wheelchair; freedom.

Realizing my abilities and weaknesses; acceptance.

Seeking housing and capable individuals to care for me; patience.

Coming to Charlottesville, children moved into their room; we're home.

It's been over six months … Thank you Lord … Determination!

Echoes

Listen closely...

To the cries of the fallen

To the moans of the frail and ill

To wailing of the depressed and lonely

Render a heart - felt prayer for speedy healing

Assist in the rebuilding and restoration of warm dreams

Lend a helping hand, a listening ear and a miraculous inspiring smile

Be very kind always; you never know how the simplest jesters can be uplifting

GOD SAID

We need to love one another

Our life has not been in vain

Repent your sin through prayer

Serve ME with your whole heart

Heed MY word and pattern your actions accordingly

Include ME in all that you do

Praise ME for all your experiences

The formula is: W + O + R + S + H + I + P = Eternal Life

AMEN

The Meaning of Christmas

In more ways than I knew, WE honor Christ at Christmas

Of course we all know and recreate the birth with the Nativity

Even though most aren't Jewish, we begin our celebrations of the Lord at least 7 days before Christmas

I didn't know the meaning of some usual practices until now…

Did you know the chopping down of a tree represents Christ dying on the Cross?

The act of taking it home and standing it back up, represents the resurrection

Even the wreath on the door represents the eternal life… the never ending circle

Maybe this is why it feels good to decorate for Christmas

Even candy canes have significance, they're fashioned like a shepherd's Crook

Don't get tripped up by the name of the stick

Candy cane makers purposely dropped the hook at the end

The colors red for the blood and wte of purity

The gifts represents the offerings of the wise men to baby Jesus

So this year and going forward don't worry over finding that perfect gift

We've had it all along

Jesus Christ was given to US to atone for our sins…

So let's put Christ back in Christmas!

Hair don't make the Person

An adult woman has about 5 million hair follicles on her body

Men have about a hundred thousand more

Hair is distributed evenly with the exception of hairless palms and soles

At birth 100,000 of those follicles are on your head, whew thank God for baby hairs!

Do blondes have more fun? A natural blond is estimated to have 150,000 scalp hairs

Most adults have 100-110,000 scalp follicles but not brown or black hair color... 10,000 less,

The more follicles the least intelligent... ditzy blond?

Rumor? Truth? This is how easy prejudices can grow... faster than a single strand

What if you lose your hair? Sampson believed his strength was tied to his hair

Chemo robs, so does old age levels the playing field... everyone eventually grays

We pity those that lose their hair because of illness... view them as weak

Admire someone who chooses to go clean shaven, see them as Virile

What message are we sending? Does hair make the man? What about the woman that loses her hair?

I say shave the world bald for a year and ask that question again...

Better yet just sit back and observe.... not having to cut, style and shampoo daily is freeing

The average person spends thirty minutes a day on haircare, 5475 hours a year on grooming our locks

Embrace your inner baldness!

What am I supposed to do NOW?

Now that I can't pick up the phone to tell you about the crazy day I had,

I still hear you laughing, saying at least you had a day, so many didn't wake up today.

Okay so now you've gone and joined that group, I had so much left to say to you

We never think today will be my last time to say be safe, I love you!

Everyone gets lost in the daily grinds, the hustle and bustle of work, school and life

No one means to look up and realize 3 years have slipped by since that last conversation.

A fleeting thought gets pushed for that perfect time later; after work, after dinner, after the kids are asleep

The next thing you know its tomorrow, the grind begins again.

With that fleeting thought you smile, say a prayer and vow to call later

Unfortunately later never came

So I've been reduced to tears, regret and memories

Wishing life hadn't gotten too busy to live and enjoy with those that mattered…

In loving memory of those friends and family gone on to Glory,

You've got to Heal Yourself

We all began from the union of our parents DNA

We are made of many complexed clusters of cells that makes up the organs

Each organ in our bodies are a part of a system and has its own functions, but can't work alone

Just like people the systems of our bodies need each other's support

The Digestive system starts at the mouth with chewing food into fuel used by the other systems

The Circulatory system is powered by the heart moving the blood flow throughout

The Respiratory system oxidizes the blood that travels to every cell

The Skeletal system holds us upright and makes every blood cell that feeds the whole body

Every choice we make for food, drink, to smoke or not; affects each cell, organ, and system

Good food and beverage choices, exercise, lots of sleep and positive thoughts are necessary

Lent and Easter are fast approaching…. what will you give up?

I'm giving up sweets; Harder than you know

Over the years I have created my own problems

Living with the knowledge that I should not indulge in greasy, highly sweetened foods

But what 17 year old can resist burgers, fries, sodas and ice cream?

Most health issues slowly begin… After my accident now immobilized; things are fast changing

They say that healing begins with acceptance and changes

God breathed life into Adam and created Eve from his rib because he saw his loneliness

He also created us in his own image so I'm choosing to reprogram my thoughts about food

I've got a lot of plans, a lot of living to do, a lot of healing and a long way to go!

Pray for me!

When I Close My Eyes

When I close my eyes while we're having a conversation I'm remembering when I was your hero, not an annoyance.

When I close my eyes while looking at you I'm carefully formulating my next comments to be totally understood.

When I close my eyes I may be wondering when I started to become a burden, March 17th twenty three years ago.

When I close my eyes sometimes I realize the pain I cause you daily because I feel the same frustrations.

When I close my eyes at night I ask God for rest, forgiveness of my transgressions and for another chance tomorrow.

When I close my eyes at night I thank God for my family, caregivers and friends.

When I close my eyes I dream of days gone by because I miss being able to go to work every day.

When I close my eyes I picture my space differently, I used to rearrange my home seasonally.

When I close my eyes that final time please remember my humor not my misgivings.

When I close my eyes that final time I will have no regrets, I've had a blessed life.

When I close my eyes that final time don't cry for me, don't forget me and don't let go of each other.

When I close my eyes that final time please know I tried to show my love always.

Forgive me for being human I didn't get it right every time!

Waxing Nostalgic

Summer slowly fades to fall

Basketball tournament ends

Leaves dwindle down, branches are bare

Warm breezes sharply turn brisk, bitter and bone chillingly cold

The last hot air balloon rises over Fox-field races

Halloween right around the corner… trick or treaters

Thanksgiving, Black Friday craziness

Then that mad dash for that illusive toy that every child on the planet wants

Finding that perfect mother "shut-up" gift… that she'll flip over

Wrapping gifts at midnight after finally shooing the kids to bed

Checking for batteries in everything before placing under the Christmas tree

Turkey into oven before retiring for a long over-do nap

Six comes too soon…. Overzealous shaking by children screaming "Santa came, come on"

Pretending to be awake enough to be happy about what everyone received

Cinnamon buns and eggs for breakfast…. sugar high to crash and burn by 2pm

Turkey dinner with all the fixings, everybody ready for bed by 6…

Another Christmas done… another year almost gone!

The Climate is changing!

It's November 20, 2021 and the leaves are confused also

Some haven't changed colors or fallen

Yesterday 70 degrees and looking like spring

Today pneumonia weather, struggling to get to the 40's.

People have become as iffy as the weather

Scammers at every turn, hard to trust

Even Politicians with personal agendas before the needs of America

Parties fighting within themselves.

Everywhere you look the trees are disappearing

Polar ice caps are melting

Animals are losing natural sanctuaries

Our furry friends are prettier in the wild not in our streets

The bears, the deer or rabbits can't make changes but we can reduce, recycle and reuse

Replace plastic straws with reusable metal ones

Restore the forest and clean up behind ourselves

Reducing our Carbon footprint isn't hard, but it takes a little effort from all us!

Let's leave a healthier planet to our grandchildren than we inherited!

The many faces of Kim

Before the ulcers ensues I need to work on me…

Me inside want to understand, help and forgive that's the Christian way

The patient in me was truly lucky that family was in house today; abandonment is real and dangerous

The boss in me is in turmoil with the other faces, I struggle with keeping the personal me out of the job

The lone woman on this island has attachment issues and befriends everyone

The human side wants to be friendly and that causes problems when it's time to separate, discipline or fire

How do I teach all of my faces to put on a stiff upper lip, a strong suit of armor or not care at the risk of myself?

I always find too many cheeks to turn, I need to find a happy medium

What I've learned today is that I need to put all of my faces first and pray about feeling guilty later

I have enough abdominal problems to deal with already

Praying for mental clarity for everyone!

Unfinished

Why is it apparent to everyone except us?

The nothing conversations that weren't really necessary

The birthday phone calls every year and the heartbreak for days after

Wishing for a time machine, wanting a do-over

Hating that I didn't fight hoping that time would heal, longing for the right words

It's hard on all that tried to penetrate the heart that belonged to another

Going through the motions with an elephant in the bedroom

Wondering even now if love could be enough….The elephant has changed

Will the past be enough to resurrect the true feelings?

Can you see pass the wheelchair and remember the ME that made you smile, laugh and care?

Can we build from right now or from that moment in my hospital room?

Yes I will need your help and others…. don't decide fast, but think carefully

Ask your family, ask your heart…. I still love you!

Whatever Happened to

To neighbors that cared enough about their neighborhood to help keep it clean

Clean enough for children to feel safe

Safe enough for the elderly to walk alone the first week of any given month

I so want that neighborhood that doesn't need the be protected by law enforcement

I would like to attend another block party to celebrate the graduates

Instead of the neighborhood meeting because someone's child is missing

I wish we could go back to the "Mayberry townspeople way", where everyone says HELLO

Where people pitched in the do chores like cutting grass, painting or errands for the sick or shut-in

To carry a pie to a newcomer and say "welcome", you'll love living here

Not worrying are my children safe next door to the grumpy man that never waves or speaks

I want in before dark to be by choice not because of fear

I long to hear children laughing as they play in the gush of a fire hydrant's stream

I miss the good old days of yesterday

When life was simpler, time moved slower and WE were calmer

Nothing made us go from zero to ballistic in mere seconds

When we didn't shoot first then ask why

Love thy neighbor meant something other than bed his wife while he's working

YES this is MY wish for yesteryear's morals today…Ranting again!

Over There

I've always been told that it's beautiful beyond belief, over there

I have family I never met, over there

I have friends and pets…. over there

I want to meet Jesus and sit in awe of God, over there

I try to live my life here to be able to make it over there

Over there where the streets are paved with gold

Over there where we won't need wheelchairs

Over there where arthritis and paralysis doesn't exist

Over there where color don't matter

Over where everyone speaks the same language

Over there's where we need not worry about money, health or dangers

Over there's where our only job is to praise God

Glory! Glory! Hallelujah….. Over there!

Only the Strong Survive

Every living thing will face adversity, how we handle the things we're challenged by is key…

Be like the Camel learn to walk across the hot sands of life

Be like a Cactus learn to survive standing in heat of day and the chill after sundown

Become a Turtle wear your shell wholeheartedly and know it'll protect you

Become an Ant… the hardest working creature on earth

Even the Cockroach has been surviving for a million years

I'm a survivor because I keep my eyes on Glory

I'm a survivor because I believe God isn't done with ME

Giving up is not an option!

By the Grace of God we're given another chance every morning!

One hundred million words….

Won't be enough syllables to describe the best sunrise after a hurricane

Or the clean air after a volcanic eruption

Never underestimate the value of a cool breeze on a sweltering day

Revel in the calm.

There's never enough words to describe the miracle of child birth

Rejoice in transitioning and cry for the babies just starting this journey

We've all been given a blessing every morning

Don't waste a moment.

Enjoy the rooster's crow, the duck's quack and the cow's moo

For these animals give us entertainment and food

Heed the dog's bark, the rattle snake's jingle and a cat's hiss

Danger surely announces itself.

No matter the conversation with death; the outcome is terminal

Put your affairs in order, make your wishes known

Don't burden your loved ones with final calls

Rest easy; the living is done!

No fan of Mondays

Monday morning rolls around too soon

Corporate America starts the week at nine a.m. on Mondays

No one wants to realize Sunday as the first day of the week even though the calendar does

Christians know that the Sabbath begins the week

On Sunday's we should thank God for seeing another day, the close of last week and guidance for the future

We should also pray for upcoming endeavors, for the world, for coworkers and family

As we retire on Sunday evening we should try to reset our mindset or maybe it's just me…

Naw! I observe others dragging on Mondays

Maybe they're sad that the weekend is over, maybe they didn't know Monday was the second day of the week

Maybe it's not Monday that depresses; maybe it's having to deal with others…

If you're not fortunate enough to work with Monday people change your attitude about the first day of the week

Mondays will continue to come by God's grace!

Change what you can control…. YOU!

Licensing

I had to take a written test to be allowed to take the on the road exam for a driver's license

Another test and OTR training for a CDL

You even need a license to fish

I also had to license both cats and the dog

To be a nurse you have to renew your license every two years or retest

Even hairdressers, barbers and or cosmetologists have to be licensed

So why doesn't the most important job in the world at least require testing

Any female with a womb and a desire can pop out a child

Despite temperament abilities or deserving

Never mind the fact that two children died suspiciously at bath time in previous years

I realize that most parents try to raise their children to be productive well-rounded individuals

This rant is about the unfit, lazy, abusive few that shouldn't be allowed a goldfish

Children are our future…

Future doctors, political leaders, future parents

Children live what they learn…

They mimic their role models, what are you teaching those that are watching?

<u>I want it to be Christmas already</u>

Cold weather but warm hearts

People seem nicer over all, hi and excuse me flows freer

Children are more behaved

Lights and holly wreaths decorates every house or apartment's door

The aroma of evergreen or pine in the living room

Cookies, turkey and sweet potato pies waft upstairs

Secretly listening to every conversation between your parents trying to hear what you're getting

Shopping up to Christmas Eve looking for bargains and that special something for everyone

Decorating a little every day after Halloween

Hiding in your room to wrap the trinkets, baubles and treasures you're gifting

Baking cookies for Santa, leaving carrots and apples for the reindeer

Praying for Santa's safe ride with your children as you tuck them in….

Anything to sell the fantasy!

DON'T tell me there's no GOD

A very well respected female supervisor shocked me by saying there's no GOD

I didn't understand this statement from her and asked her to defend her view

I went on to say I believe that my higher power wakes me every morning

She said it was my alarm clock

I said Jesus kept us close and in our right minds

She said Alzheimer will soon steal that mindset like a thief in the night

I pointed to a field of wild flowers, all she could see was the cause of allergies

After thinking for a bit about our conversation I decided something must have happened

I then remembered the night of my accident and I said…

If there's no God then I was protected by my guardian angel because someone calmed me

A soothing hand touched my cheek when I wanted to sit up and move

Before I could say another word I saw a tear trickle down her face and she said…

I lost my mom two days ago and I didn't get to say good bye but I now know she's at peace

I was frustrated because I didn't get an immediate answer

Your story gave me confirmation to a prayer from that day, thank you!

I was confused about the transformation for a moment but then…

I realized **GOD IS REAL!**

Martin had a Dream

He was enthusiastic that we were continuing on with Abraham Lincoln's beginnings ….

That our freedom had been truly purchased by our ancestor's suffering, sacrificing and prayers

Unfortunately forward progress has been overshadowed by a powerful hatred from one influential individual

Over the last four years our nation's attitude, acceptance and tolerance has become deplorable

Prayers that our people would no longer be enslaved, persecuted and denied have seemingly stopped

Denial of our rights… victimized by those charged to protect and serve; enslavement by idiotic individuals has risen,

Persecution because someone else is uncomfortable with the color of our skin isn't hidden under hoods today

When the vibe of the capital became toxic it spread throughout the nation

Martin's dream is definitely suffering but it doesn't have to die here

We as humans need to become the caring loving and giving people that we'd like our neighbors to be

America was founded to escape religious tyranny and to be the controller of our civil liberties

Not only is Martin's dream on life support, so is the Pilgrim's

Thankfully there's hope on the horizon

A changing of the "guard" in Washington D.C. and a renewed attention to the overall health of the nation

An infusion of positive and motivated ideologies on the state levels

BUT the biggest change must happen within individual's heart…

Let's revive Martin's dream!

I SCREAMED NO

When he rolled up on me with his weak rap,

I knew he wasn't worth my time.

He couldn't believe someone wasn't falling for his baby blues and Polo cologne

"I just want to know the name of the prettiest girl in the world" he continued

Nunya I replied, he chuckled "you got jokes"

I got to go, my shift starts in 10.

I could tell NO wasn't something he could understand, so I quickened my pace

Trying to hurry from the dimly lit parking garage

If the elevator will open fast enough

Please be occupied… there's safety in numbers

All of the training in the world doesn't help against a rapist's attacks

I tried to stab with my keys but he knocked me down

I kicked him in the crotch but he enjoyed it rough

He drew a gun and asked "is today your dying day? ….RELAX

I couldn't leave my babies without a mother

Look him eye to eye, offer myself to him, be attentive and loving

Take the wind out of his sail, survive by any means necessary

Get into it moan, scream but never cry

Engage his member, grab it tightly to smear the DNA

Scratch his back deeply, make mental notes of time and location

Pray that it ends soon, pray he keeps his word…

SURVIVE just SURVIVE!

Because of Love

Knowing He was royalty, He still labored as a carpenter.

Knowing He would be persecuted, He still taught about salvation.

Knowing He would be beaten and bruised, He still gave the blind man sight.

Knowing He would be crucified, He still washed their feet.

Knowing He was going to be betrayed, He still broke bread and drank with them.

Because of Love He endured the torture and accepted the crown of thorns.

Because of Love He paid for our souls on the cross.

Because of His Love we are blessed!

MICROWAVE CHRISTIAN

What does this mean? I'm going to tell you.

The kind that can judge you but see no fault within.

The one that claims GOD in their summer season, but complaints when it's cold.

First to volunteer for food ministries and only bring enough for immediate family.

Fired up for causes until they're asked to contribute time or financially.

Don't mind doing things that get themselves recognition.

Can quote key passages of the BIBLE, but don't know why JESUS wept.

Cursing, drinking, and gambling on Saturday nights, but in church on Sunday morning

The true question is do I fit in one of these categories?

If so LORD, Please fix me…AMEN!!!

Freedom 101

I wanted to know if I was living with the freedoms our ancestors dreamt of, so...

I started by finding the meaning of freedom: the state of being free or unrestricted political liberties

Another source called it exemption from external control, interference, regulation, etc.

Even further exploring lead to this: personal liberty, as opposed to bondage or slavery

Although great meanings, the thing that stood out most was how each source pronounced freedom (free-duh m)

In my mind (duh) has always meant oh really, not exactly or NO!

The first part (free-) may match the upper definitions but (-dom) in computer language means dominion or domain

So doesn't this make the word freedom an oxymoron?

We may not still have leg irons but have we really broken the shackles?

We've come a long way but as Robert Frost said:

"Miles to go before we sleep"

ABC's of a Real Woman

A real woman will always be confident because she'll live her authentic self.

A real woman will be loyal because she'll never betray love ones.

A real woman will always be considerate because she knows compassion.

A real woman will acknowledge your feelings because she'll know the value of a decent mate.

A real woman will protect children because she'll know the importance of family.

A real woman will conduct her affairs with grace because she loves God.

A real woman is caring because she knows humility and will love hard because it fuels her soul.

A real woman will never believe gossip without proof because she's intelligent.

A real woman will not be naïve because she'll know that jealousy is a warning sign not an emotion.

A real woman will work hard to provide but not be consumed by the need for money.

A real woman will be confident enough to rock braids, perms, or a natural.

A real woman will dream, strive and plan for the future because she's optimistic.

A real woman will never be broke because she lives up to her potential.

A real woman will take care of her belongings because she values quality.

A real woman will remember the past, learn from it but not try to avenge it because she's rational.

A real woman will rebuild after being broken because she has stamina.

A real woman knows how to turn a tragedy into a triumph. A real woman isn't a slave to fashion because she's unique.

A real woman is vibrant because she has a vision for life's enjoyment.

A real woman is always successful because of a strong willingness to try again and again.

A real woman never needs to explain her choices. A real woman will yearn for knowledge and peace.

A real woman will love the Lord because of her zeal to be righteous.

If you have such a woman with half of these qualities you have someone special cherish her!

The ABC's of a Real Man

A real man will never be poor because he is ambitious. A real man won't disrespect his lady because he's not brazen!

A real man will succeed because of his confidence.

A real man will not fail because of his determination.

A real man will achieve because he is energetic. A real man will be successful because of his fortitude.

A real man will be humbled because of gratitude.

A real man will kneel to pray because he's humble.

A real man will ask for help because he's intelligent. A real man will be gentle because he's not jealous.

A real man will be educated because he seeks knowledge.

A real man will be funny because he enjoys laughter.

A real man will be interesting because he's metrosexual.

A real man will handle any situation because he's not naive. A real man will be happy because he's optimistic.

A real man will never be pessimistic because he sees potential.

A real man will find answers because he will question.

A real man will observe because he's reserved.

A real man will go to church because he's spiritual.

A real man will be peaceful because he has tolerance. A real man will be mysterious because he's unique.

A real man will fight for his lady because he's valiant.

A real man will love hard because he's wonderful.

A real man will be a provider because he's exuberant. A real man will explore because he's yearning.

A real man will never be lazy because he has zeal.

If you have someone with half of these qualities he's on his way. Groom, support, and love him into your best real man!

Haiku fun

Winter Chill

A bite in the air

The last leaves have fallen now

Tis no longer fall!

Easter

Cute family outfits

Grass stains and patent leather

Hidden eggs search!

July 4th

Celebrating freedom now

Fireworks light the sky!

Cookout before dark

Thanksgiving

Turkey and gravy

Family from far and wide

A Celebration!

Christmas

Some happy children

Lots of noisy toys around

Tired, happy parents!

New Year's Day

Broken Resolutions

Black eye pea dinner tonight

Work again tomorrow!

That Little A-Frame House

Held lots of Dreams, Growth, Love, and Secrets.

The three bedrooms were as different as the paint that adorned the walls.

The upstairs powder blue didn't represent boys, quite the contrary, four graceful daughters.

The pine paneled bedroom truly represented the three brothers that inhabited it.

The master doubled as the feminine hangout spot on football Sundays.

I remember the lady of the house's favorite perch having the perfect vantage point.

The heart and soul of any home is the kitchen, I spent many good times there.

Like most kitchens it held many gatherings most festive and happy, but a few sad.

Like any house eventually the family grows up and leaves nothing but memories behind.

Soon there's nothing left of that little A-frame house except the vacant lot where love lived.

<u>I'm sure you think...</u>

That because you don't remember me picking you up when you were crying or afraid, that I never did.

Far from true, I wear the scar proudly.

That because I wasn't there to tuck you in every night that I didn't wish you pleasant dreams.

Far from true, I asked GOD to send special angels to watch over you.

That because I'm not the one that put you on the school bus your first day, that I didn't care.

Far from true, I prayed you would meet your best friend that day.

That because I missed all of the times you scored a touchdown that I couldn't care less.

Far from true, I prayed for protection, agility, and stamina.

Yes there's so many things that I didn't get to witness, or experience with you. For this I'm sorry.

But there's one thing I never missed, and that's a night from thanking GOD for you.

Dedicated to my first born son, I love you all EQUALLY!!!

Looking

Every one of us, at some point in our lives stop to take a look, in many different directions.

We look back to mark the passing of time and remember the good old days of youthfulness.

We look back to acknowledge growth and to reminisce on what we have overcome.

We look back quite often to remember, in the attempt not to repeat the past mistakes.

We look at right now asking am I happy, content, and fulfilled with my life as it is?

We look at this moment, wondering have we achieved every goal we have dreamt.

We look at today to assess our present situation and formulate a plan for the future.

We look forward to the promises of GOD!

GIVING

When most think of giving the first thoughts go to Birthday and Christmas gifts.

A second and deeper thought may remind you of advice or time you've given your family.

An even closer look recalls charitable donations of clothing, food, and also buying from pint- sized peddlers.

Another moment of pondering will bring your thoughts to my true subject….money

Depending on your financial status, the words used to describe money can be very different.

The financially wealthy upper-crust may refer to it as a "C-note", "Commodities", "Futures" and even a "Stock portfolio".

The middle class are between two very different cultures, so they can pick and choose the terms that fits the situation.

The less financially stable call it "Benjamins", "Cabbage", "Cheddar", and even "Duckies", but rarely ever a dollar.

Have you ever noticed the weird looks people gives someone who wants to write a check for purchases anywhere?

It's as if you just asked the cashier for paper bags in the supermarket, then demanded double bagging & lightly filled.

If you can't charge it, deliver it, order it, scan it, slide it, swipe it, or waive it, Americans can't seem to pay for things.

The Dollar bill is not just becoming soft, it's becoming a relic; do our children still learn to give change in school?

For education and fascination of my grandson, we searched for the 10 most widely used forms of currency worldwide.

The U.S $1 topped the list @ 87%, and I can't help but wonder if it's because we will buy from anyone and anywhere.

Speaking from experience, I love giving. I've heard and read that GOD loves a cheerful giving soul.

Therefore, I will continue to give to charities, family, friends, and especially to GOD by praise and tithing.

Happiness

That elusive drug, an emotional high.

No heron, marijuana or booze can compare.

This fluttering in my heart and daydreams that linger.

When you catch yourself smiling and don't know why.

The coldest day of winter can't chill that yearning.

Happiness is being in Love!

Life's Tapestry

Woven together strand by strand, year by year.

Woven with the rich reds of anticipation.

Woven will the bold blues of disappointment.

Woven with the vibrant yellows of desire.

Woven with the great greens of potential.

Woven with the pure white of life.

Woven with the melancholy black of demise.

Each generation adds its threads to this tapestry.

My Assets

My piggybank contains less than 100 coins, unfortunately they're mostly pennies.

My checking account has sixty dollars, but I still have $75 of bills to pay and food to buy.

My savings account was started 30+ years ago as a backup plan, all I've saved is a $500 deductible.

Yes on paper my situation looks bleak, but I know I'm going to receive my richest rewards in Heaven.

Not one day have I ever went hungry from lack of food, nor have I longed for shelter or companionship.

Sometimes we're fast to complain because things are not as comfortable as we wish, but we're blessed.

I wish sometimes that I didn't have to pay rent, but then I thank GOD for my apartment and comfortable bed.

Sometimes we complain we're tired of eating the same old things always, right then I thank GOD for a full belly.

Sometimes I get bored with my life; in bed more than out, its then that I'm reminded just how blessed I am to be here.

So the equation for my assess reads: (SSI-BILLS) + GOD = Paid in Full…

My Make Up

My makeup doesn't come from a cylinder with a brush to thicken my eyelashes.

My makeup isn't a powder in a box to be applied by sponge for blushing cheeks.

My makeup cannot be applied from a tube to accent my pretty perky pucker.

My makeup is much deeper than my complexion or outward facial image.

My eyes should be looked at during conversation, because they indicate truth or deceit.

My cheeks should be observed during encounters for they express emotions.

My lips should be carefully listened to, because I'll only speak the truth and encouragement.

My inner makeup is what determines my overall worth: My makeup is SINCERITY!

OMG is the most widely used phrase in today's language all across the globe.

To me OMG stands for Oh my God

I will tell you why OMG stands for Oh my God to me:

Oh my God can do anything but fail

Oh my God wakes me up every morning closed in my right mind

Oh my God there were mornings I was not closed in my right mind but my God did not leave me there

Oh my God he saved me from a horrific car accident that could have taken my life

Oh my God has healed me from many illnesses that could have taken me out

Oh my God has kept me even when I didn't even know him he protected me

Oh my God has covered to me, carried me and ordered my steps

Oh my God has blessed me with three children and allow me to see them grow into manhood

Oh my God is wonderful, gracious, and merciful and worthy to be PRAISED!

AMEN

No Regrets

Every day should be met with anticipation.

Good days bring happiness, bad leave a longing of hope.

Both shape your character and strengthen your resolve.

Happiness generates a euphoric smile and warms the heart.

Trouble makes us work that much harder and long for peace.

Happiness and sorrow are human emotions.

Success or failure are results of effort.

Never look back in regret, each experience fosters growth.

Revenge

Boy chases sister with scissors to cut her golden locks.

Redemption.

Sister outs brother.

Folks say "revenge is a dish best served cold."

So is Gazpacho.

Sunrise

Vibrant yellow rays from a brick red sun.

Billowy white puffy clouds.

Is this the sunrise GOD sees daily?

Is this what Heaven looks like?

Or is it just the picture on my wall?

Believing!

Unforgiven

How could you be so selfish?

Depressed, no will to live; checking out.

Why me, why the students and the cop?

Scared to go alone; taking as many as you can.

You insured their passage to Glory!

And your descent to Hell!

Praying for the survivors!

Made in the USA
Columbia, SC
01 July 2022